MOTIVATE THIS

MOTIVATE THIS
The Simple Approach to Motivation

Vinny Verelli
The Goomba Guru of
Negativity Management[SM]

WORKBOOK EDITION

Atlanta

Jon Schwartz
Bacchus Press
2095-A General Truman Street
Atlanta, GA 30318
Jon@bacchusprod.com

FIRST EDITION

Printed in the United States of America
Library of Congress Control Number: 2004111857
ISBN: 0-9761173-0-4

Cover design by Eric Key
Cover photo by Sheri Besher
Caricatures by Patrick Trujilo
Edited by Amy Crownover

www.motivatethis.net

For
Erv & Lee
and
That Palm Reader
in Old San Juan

CONTENTS

ACKNOWLEDGMENTS

They said this would be the place to, you know, thank people who helped me to get this book out.

A lot of people said, "Vinny, you writing a book? I didn't know you could read." I also got encouragement from my wife – anything to keep me from talking during *Everybody Loves Raymond*: "Vinny, go write your book." Although everyone was polite: "Oh, what's it about?" I'd tell them and they would smile.

The only person who believed in the book, believed in me, from the beginning, was my editor and good friend, Amy Crownover. If it were up to me, I would have published anything just to have something to put in my promotional kit. She kept me focused and honest and, at the same time, gave the book a structure. Most of all, Amy gave me encouragement; she made me feel like I could write. For this I'll always be grateful. Of course, if this book stinks…well, that doesn't say too much for Amy now, does it?

I have to thank Amy's husband…I think his name is Dean. Thanks, Dean, for letting Amy work for margaritas. I'll make it up to you guys, I promise.

Vinny Verelli   ix

Thanks also go out to Vince Tortorici and Barry Stoltze who read the manuscript of this book and didn't laugh at me; they laughed at the material. That gave me encouragement, also. And these guys gave some good suggestions.

Much thanks to Dan Fahey for helping document Vinny's early speaking career. I told Dan I'd put his name in the Acknowledgments if he didn't show tape of the speech I gave at a Kiwanis Club in Clayton County, Georgia.

I want to thank the National Speakers Association for allowing me to become a member and for welcoming me with open arms. I especially want to thank everyone at the Georgia Chapter of NSA...well, not everyone; I mean, I don't even know everyone. I want to thank all the people I do know for their willingness to help.

I owe so much to Dan Thurmon, CSP, for being there to listen to me and give good advice. He was a good friend long before he became my personal mentor on call. Everyone wants to give you advice, but Dan knew me, knew where I was coming from and was able to give me balanced guidance. Thanks, Dan.

If I forgot anyone...tough. You should have done more.

MOTIVATE THIS

INTRODUCTION

After carving my slice out of the motivational speaking pie, I realized, hey, I like pie. I'll never give up cannolis but I want more pie. Motivational books and tapes are where it's at – and, by making this book a workbook, I can charge you for pie *a la mode*.

There are as many motivational and self-help books on the shelf these days as diet books – which means one of two things: the world is one big, pathetic, helpless crowd, or you people will buy anything. Either way, I wanted to pontificate (putting my *Verbal Advantage*® skills to work), and I figured that if I could get paid to mouth off, that would be a good thing.

The opinions expressed in this book are my own, so you can't blame anyone else. This book, I hope, will make you think, make you laugh, and make you want to buy a sequel.

By the way, I would appreciate your comments. You know, about what I say in this book and/or your own thoughts on any given topic. If I get enough responses, then I can compile them all and...bada bing...there's my sequel. I love this country.

PART I:

The Birth of a Motivational Speaker

Success is how high you bounce when you hit bottom.
— George Smith Patton

An Auspicious Beginning

When I was sixteen, I dropped out of school. To be more truthful, I would have to say that I was "drop-kicked" out of school. As I look back, I realize that it was the best thing that ever happened to me. *No, not really. The best thing would have to be the Gambino Twins in 1979.* What I mean to say is that if I had stayed in school, I would have had a high school diploma (maybe) but no job. Leaving school in the tenth grade gave me a jump on the other bums growing up in my neighborhood.

The actual incident that caused my expulsion from Our Lady of Perpetual Misery was somewhat prophetic. Let me explain. Mickey O'Connor and I were trading punches from our desks. You know, taking turns hitting each other in the arm as hard as we could. You keep punching each other until one person quits or the bell rings. This is something we did every afternoon in History class.

We didn't choose History class for our sport because we weren't interested in the past; we chose it because Sister Mary Margaret was as blind as a bat. She could see her books and the blackboard, but as long as Mickey and I weren't too loud, she never saw us.

I gave Mickey what I considered to be the winning punch. I mean, he had a welt growing on his arm and his eyes were starting to tear up. End of game, right? No. Behind the tears I could see the fire and determination. I knew I was in for it. He leaned over his desk to get more leverage. He reared back for more force. He let it fly.

I dodged the punch. Needless to say, Mickey was caught by surprise and his momentum carried him and his desk to the floor. Books, papers, and pencils flew everywhere. I nearly wet myself I was laughing so hard.

Sister Mary Margaret was not laughing. I guess all the commotion set off her bat-radar or something. She made her way to the site of the action, brandishing her ruler like a battle-ax. She beat the crap out of both of us, and then gave us a lecture. She told us that we would be lucky to get out of the tenth grade – that we'd never amount to anything; we'd be bums the rest of our lives. For a near-sighted nun, she had no problem seeing into the future.

Then she said we weren't motivated. I felt I was extremely motivated, just not in the things Sister Mary Margaret thought were important. She said we didn't appreciate the work the sisters were doing, that the sisters were there to teach and to motivate us. That's when I said, "Motivate this."

That earned me one of the best laughs ever. It also got me expelled. It was the last time I told a joke at school and the only time I got sucker-punched by a nun. To this day, I never get within an arm's length of anyone wearing a habit or even a wimple. Or penguins, for that matter. *Fuhgeddaboudit!*

A journey of a thousand miles must begin with a single step.

— Lao-tzu

(or, in my case, a right hook)

Educate THIS

Education is what survives when what has been learned has been forgotten.
— B. F. Skinner

The great aim of education is not knowledge but action.
— Herbert Spencer

Education is when you read the fine print. Experience is what you get if you don't.
— Pete Seeger

I have never let my schooling interfere with my education.
— Mark Twain

It's better to be a smart man than a wise guy.
— Vinny Verelli

The Family Business

The next day found me on Grand Street in Little Italy working for my uncle's dry cleaning business. Uncle Sal was a simple businessman with a simple motto: "If it ain't ready in an hour, come back in another hour."

I spent little time at the cleaners. Most of the day and into the night found me running "errands" for my uncle. A fast and motivated "street" learner, I became an expert on finding the best route to anywhere in the city and skirting around or out of bad situations.

My best money came from working "executive" card games, high stake poker games run by some "made" guys who had a place in Tribeca. Uncle Sal arranged it. My job was simple – keep the place picked-up and get anything anybody wanted, from mixed drinks to mixed company. I kept the high rollers rolling.

Certain codes keep me from discussing anything else about these games. I'm not talking any secret family codes here, either; I'm talking penal codes. The terms of my probation keep me from divulging who attended these games, the size of the pots, or the percentage the house kept for "hosting."

As I said, I made good money. These wise guys loved to throw their money around. They tipped big and they tipped often. I didn't have a lot of ambition (or a wife and kids) in those days, so I just enjoyed the lifestyle for – twenty-six years.

Helping Others Help Themselves

I guess you could say that I was going nowhere fast. But you're never too old to change your life. One cold and wet Sunday morning, a homeless man changed mine. A homeless man and a robbery conviction.

I started walking home about 6:30 a.m. after working an all-night game. I had six "C's" in my pocket and I was feeling good.

I was on Grand between Greene and Mercer when this homeless guy came up to me asking for money. I'm really fed up with people who hit you up for money. It's not good for any city, and New York has quite a reputation.

So I asked this guy, "What do you want with my money?" He told me, "I want to get something to eat and a warm, dry place to lay down. A drink would be nice." I explained that I could arrange all of that.

I walked him over to a liquor store and instructed him on how to break the glass through the security gate and reach in to lift two bottles of XO, one for each of us. Then I told him to sit on the curb, open his bottle, and have his drink. "In about four and a half minutes," I said, "a car will come by to take you to a place that is warm and dry." Then I headed for home.

Nobody got hurt and, for the next thirty days, my friend would have free food and housing. It didn't work out exactly as planned, though, because the bum fingered me and the cops nabbed me for accessory.

> *Simplicity is the ultimate sophistication.*
> — Leonardo da Vinci

Soup to Nuts

I got off lucky since it was my first offense. Aside from the two nights in lock-up, I didn't do any real time. At the trial, I received fourteen days suspended sentence plus time served and 120 hours of community service. My service began at a soup kitchen and an after-school program working with troubled teens.

A lot of my buddies said that "doin' time" would have been the better option. My friend Joey said, "I'd rather be playing cards on Rikers than servin' soup to nuts – the filthy scum." Compassion was not something that our neighborhood held in high esteem.

In fact, I'm not sure I ever felt compassion for the people at the soup kitchen where I worked – I just decided then and there not to end up like them. I realized that I couldn't risk going back to work for my Uncle Sal or any of his friends, so I got a job delivering pizza and started downsizing my lifestyle.

I did feel a connection with the teens at the after-school program, though – they were really great. They seemed just like me at fourteen and fifteen, and they thought it was cool to be around an "adult" who knew how they felt and understood what they were going through. At the same time, I served as a big wake-up call to them. If they kept going in the same direction, they could end up like me – a forty-two-year-old dropout whose main income came from mixing drinks and emptying ashtrays for high rollers.

The experience proved to be a real wake-up call for me, too. I felt obligated to help these kids, to make sure they didn't make the same mistakes I had made. By reaching out to them, I ended up helping myself. And that's always a good thing.

Help THIS

The greatest good you can do for another is not just to share your riches, but to reveal to him his own.
— Benjamin Disraeli

Time and money spent in helping men to do more for themselves is far better than mere giving.
— Henry Ford

There is no use whatever trying to help people who do not help themselves. You cannot push anyone up a ladder unless he be willing to climb himself.
— Andrew Carnegie

Try putting a gun to his head and see how fast he climbs that ladder.
— Dante Rizzo, Vinny's cousin

From Amen to APEN

Forever looking for human-interest stories, a reporter for the *New York Post* heard about my work with troubled teens and decided to write about me – a goomba turned do-gooder. I told him all about my misguided youth and how my buddies and I used to hassle the people out on Sheepshead Bay – nothing serious, just calling out and making obscene gestures and all.

Being a native New Yorker himself, the reporter related to my story. He asked me to write a guide to Sheepshead Bay for newcomers, telling people my favorite spots – like which bars have the best steamed mussels, the best Clams Casino, the best Chianti, or the coldest beer. I also included information on how to deal with the bums that hang out on the street. Finally, my knowledge of the streets was put to good use.

It just so happens that someone from APEN read the article and invited me to write travel brochures for them. APEN, which stands for Accentuate the Positive, Eliminate the Negative, is an organization made up of New Yorkers from all walks of life. We combine our diverse backgrounds to form a single, unified team that strives to enhance New York City's image by eliminating the negative.

Just like the New York Convention and Visitors Bureau and the Chamber of Commerce, we provide visitors to New York City with travel guides. The difference is that we write no-nonsense guides that accentuate the positive aspects of the city (of course) but more importantly, we don't pretend there are no negatives. We tell visitors how to avoid – or at least how to deal with – the negative should they come face-to-face with it.

During this time at APEN, I developed my theory of Negativity Management. (I'll explain this concept in detail during the "content" portion of this book.) As I wrote travel guides, it became obvious to me that the principles of Negativity Management could be applied to our personal and business lives. Thus, my motivational philosophy was born. And copyrighted. Soon I was being asked to speak to all the service organizations and then the paid engagements rolled in.

So, guess what, Sister Mary Margaret? Thirty-five years after you told me I wasn't motivated, I'm a motivational speaker! That's what you call irony.

But, I don't really expect this book to motivate you, the reader. After all, you didn't pay that much for it.

PART II:

Who Moved My Brain

For every man there exists a bait which he cannot
resist swallowing.

— Friedrich Nietzsche

Inspire THIS

Where the willingness is great, the difficulties cannot be great.

— Niccolo Machiavelli

A man will fight harder for his interests than for his rights.

— Napoleon Bonaparte

Motivation is a fire from within. If someone else tries to light that fire under you, chances are it will burn very briefly.

— Stephen R. Covey

People often say that motivation doesn't last.
Well, neither does bathing – that's why we recommend it daily.

— Zig Ziglar

Unless someone like you cares a whole awful lot, nothing is going to get better. It's not.

— Dr. Seuss

I often get asked the question, "Vinny, what made you decide to become a motivational speaker?" More often I'm asked, "Vinny, you're a motivational speaker?" I would have to say that it was Tony Robbins who "motivated" me to give it a shot.

Limited Wisdom, Unlimited Word Count

Everybody has heard of Tony Robbins, the mega-guru of the motivational world. Robbins' first book *Unlimited Power* has been translated into fourteen languages and over a million copies have been sold.

But if Tony Robbins is so good, if *Unlimited Power* was so great…why did he have to write all those other books? Why are there *Personal Power I* and *Personal Power II, Power Talk I* and *Power Talk II* – and *Unleash the Power Within*? Okay, I'll admit that last title caught even my attention. All these books tell me that either Robbins hasn't gotten it right yet or, like I said earlier, you people will buy anything. Robbins has sold over twenty-four million tapes – and he's just the tip of the iceberg. Can you say "pie"?

The shelf space devoted to self-help books continues to grow at an alarming pace. I believe it's growing at an equal rate to the increased number of people on Prozac. Let me explain. You buy a motivational book, and what happens? You get motivated. After a while, you start to lose that motivation. You get depressed, you take Prozac, you buy another book.

Aside from all the books and tapes, there's got to be over a thousand motivational speakers out there. A thousand different people all saying the same thing: "Get off your butt and do something!" Now, for some people, that may be all they need to get motivated – for about ten minutes.

Motivational books and philosophies have been around for quite some time. Robert Collier's *The Secret of the Ages* was first published in 1926. In 1937, Napoleon Hill put down in writing the gospel according to Andrew Carnegie in his book *Think and Grow Rich*.

Napoleon Hill spent twenty years researching and developing Carnegie's formula for obtaining wealth. Today, people won't devote twenty minutes to understand a simple concept. Now everything is "Hurry up!" People still want to be motivated, but they say, "Motivate me now, I have a lunch at one."

My paperback edition of *The Power of Positive Thinking* is 209 pages with tiny print. On the other hand, *Who Moved My Cheese* is 94 pages with big print – and lots of pictures. Do you see where I'm going with this? I didn't think so.

What I'm trying to say is, we don't have time for Twelve Steps any more and Seven Habits take way too long to master. These days, we can sort all people into four personality types and manage things...bada bing... just like that, in one minute. (Right now many of you are measuring the size of this print and flipping to the back of the book to see how many pages it has. Too late, somebody already bought it.)

Time Manage THIS

Time is what we want most, but...what we use worst.
— William Penn

The Present is a Point just passed.
— David Russell

It is never too late to be what you might have been.
— George Eliot

The only thing that has to be finished by next Tuesday is next Monday.
— Jennifer Yane

How long a minute is, depends on which side of the bathroom door you're on.
— Zall's Second Law

The Tao of Vinny vs. the Tao of Pooh

What's worse than being spoon-fed one-minute motivation techniques? Being spoon-fed by cartoon characters and terrible parables. Now, I'm not highly educated, but I don't need Winnie the *frickin'* Pooh to tell me how to solve my problems, okay? I don't need some mice and little people in a maze running around to tell me how to adapt to change. First of all, I don't even *like* cheese. But if I did, you don't touch my cheese, yet alone move it. *Capice*?

Some people change when they see the light, others when they feel the heat.
— Caroline Schoeder

Lactose Intolerant

You know, not once during this cheesy book did the author ever address the underlying question: Who DID move the cheese? The stupid book is called *Who Moved My Cheese*, right? That's the first thing I wanted to know! Who is this "person" who toys with us to see who adapts better to change?

My wife, Sophia, she thinks the "person" is God. She says that it's obvious that there is some higher being watching over the maze and He is the one moving the cheese: "If the cheese is a metaphor for those things we desire," she says, "then so, too, is the person moving the cheese a metaphor. The only person who has this kind of power over us is God." Obviously, Sophia has never spent any time in the business sector.

I Ain't Bitin'

Let's cut the cheese and talk about sea life. What's with all the "Fish" books? There are *Fish!*, *Fish! Tales*, *Fish! Sticks,* and *Whale Done!* We learn how to bring fun into the workplace by studying fishmongers in Seattle and learn compassionate and successful management skills from Shamu, the Killer Whale.

Growing up, my father used to tell us a "fish story." He told my brother and me that little boys should obey their parents and be good to other people. Bad boys would end up like Lucca Brazzi – who sleeps with the fishes. End of discussion. *Fuhgeddaboudit.*

> *Progress is impossible without change, and those who cannot change their minds cannot change anything.*
> — George Bernard Shaw

Don't Kid Yourself

There is nothing on earth you want that you cannot have –
if only you will mentally accept the fact that you can
have it! There is nothing you cannot do – once your mind
has accepted the fact that you can do it.

— Robert Collier, *Secret of the Ages*

Robert Collier says, "When one is ready for a thing it is sure
to appear." Isn't that a lot like counting your chickens
before they hatch? This visualization stuff flies in the face
of all we've been taught.

"You can do it, you can have it all, you can get anything
you want." I'm sorry, but that kind of talk leads to
restraining orders. A truly motivated person can move
mountains, whereas the average man is only motivated
to change channels – and only when the remote is
within reach. And this is a good thing. Let's face it,
if everyone had lofty goals – if everybody was motivated,
who would pick up your garbage, flip your burgers,
wash your car?

God bless the underachiever. And God bless America,
where an average person can do well. In most countries,
underachievers starve to death. In America, the underachiever can grow up to be…President of the United States.

Visualize THIS

The person who says it can't be done should not interrupt the person doing it.

— Chinese proverb

Change your thoughts and you change your world.

— Norman Vincent Peale

What we think, we become.

— Buddha

Think you can, think you can't; either way, you'll be right.

— Henry Ford

I think I can, I think I can...

— The Little Engine That Could

PART III:

Negativity Management

What we see depends mainly on what we look for.
— John Lubbock

This section contains the "content" portion of the book and you may be compelled to skip it. However, I recommend that you do read it as it could change your life.

Make Your Blood Type B+

Regardless of whether you buy into any or all of the "Can Do" philosophies about motivation, there is one thing that all the motivational gurus agree on: a positive attitude is essential. A positive attitude is going to get you further in life than a negative one. Even if you have no goals or aspirations, even if you're a bum, you'll be a better bum if you have a positive attitude.

Achieving dreams, attaining status, accumulating large sums of money – that's all any of us really wants. So, what can you do to obtain these goals? You could win the lottery, which I know to be a major part of many people's business model. The business plan is to win the lottery. The business model is how to spend it.

While you're waiting to win the lottery, there are many books that claim they can help you. There are self-help books that cover every aspect of your life, and they all seem to have the same title. *What I want to know is, what ever happened to chicken soup for the mouth?* Just like diet books, though, none of these self-help books has the definitive answer. They all seem to work for a while, until we lose our resolve. The soup gets cold, the crackers get stale – you get the picture.

Like everything else these days, we want our motivation *right now* and the sacrifice is longevity. You may be wondering why you should bother at all if it's not going to last. And maybe you're right. But first, try *my* plan for success: Negativity Management.

I know what you're thinking: "This 'Negativity Management' sounds so, well, *negative*." You are also quick to point out that I wrote that all motivational gurus agree a positive attitude is essential. This is true, but many things stand in your way. Negativity Management helps you identify these obstacles and shove them out of the way – or at least under a bus.

Don't Miss the Bus

All these gurus of the *Think and Grow Rich* crowd leave one very important factor out of their plans: REALITY. Make no mistake, reality is the great equalizer. Reality stinks most of the time, and it never goes away. Whatever obstacles prevent you from being positive and achieving your dreams are real – and real negative. They must be managed.

The ultimate goal of Negativity Management is to eliminate all the negative things in your life. *For some of you, that's going to take a long time.* But if you apply the skills provided by this philosophy today, you can start chipping away at the negative while accentuating the positive.

Just imagine: if you eliminated all the negative things in your life, time management would be a breeze! No negatives…no conflicts to resolve. No negatives… no stress. What you do with all this new positive energy is *your* business.

Simplify THIS

The ability to simplify means to eliminate the unnecessary so that the necessary may speak.
— Hans Hofmann

To be simple is to be great.
— Ralph Waldo Emerson

Life is really simple, but we insist on making it complicated.
— Confucius

Everything should be made as simple as possible, but not simpler.
— Albert Einstein

Eat when you're hungry. Drink when you're thirsty. Sleep when you're tired.
— Buddhist proverb

(Add a 24-hour sports channel and you'll have a lot of men converting to Buddhism.)

A Simple Plan that Makes Sense

Every self-help course introduces concepts with a plan that seems to make perfect sense. Staying the course and mastering the concepts, however, is nearly impossible, leaving the reader feeling defeated and inadequate.

Everyone is afraid to fail. Failure brings with it a lot of crap that rarely goes away. We hear it all the time: "You must succeed. Failure is NOT an option." It's always, "You can do it; you must work as a team; put your back to the wheel; keep your nose to the grindstone." I'm sorry, but that just sounds painful (more unnecessary negativity). If only people wouldn't expect so much from us, right?

That's where Negativity Management comes into play. Negativity Management is better than other self-help plans because it is simple and it makes sense. It teaches us to look at a problem from the simplest perspective and then find the simplest solution.

And, the beauty of it is that you don't have to be a "master" to be successful. Most self-help books have a recipe for success that you must follow to the letter or, look out, more Prozac. In a twelve-step program, for example, you have to complete all twelve steps or you fail. Negativity Management, on the other hand, is a continual growth process. Any part of the theory you apply will help.

Raise THIS

The reason grandparents and grandchildren get along so well is that they have a common enemy.

— Sam Levenson

Call it a clan, call it a network, call it a tribe, call it a family. Whatever you call it, whoever you are, you need one.

— Jane Howard

If you cannot get rid of the family skeleton, you may as well make it dance.

— George Bernard Shaw

Happiness is having a large, loving, caring, close-knit family in another city.

— George Burns

Yeah, blood is thicker than water, but then most things are thicker than water.

— Vinny Verelli

Based on Family Values

Growing up in my family, the single, most effective motivational tool my parents wielded was FEAR.

If you did something wrong, there was no "time out." There was no "quiet time" or "talking to the hand." If you saw a hand, you better duck – and duck quick. One strike, you're out. As with Negativity Management, the rules in my family were simple, and they made sense. It's these "family" values that I've used to develop my motivational program. Let me explain.

Earlier, I mentioned that all motivational concepts and philosophies can be distilled into the one phrase: "Get off your butt and do something." Coincidentally, this was my father's motivational philosophy for my brother and me, too.

Negativity Management uses my father's saying as a mantra. Actually, it's more than a mantra; it's a command, a command that makes up my simple two-step program:

- Step 1: Get off your butt.
- Step 2: Do something!

(I'll show you how to apply my program in the "Doing the Two-Step" and workbook sections of this book.)

You see, my brother and I knew the futility of questioning anything my father said. A simple statement could become an order at any moment with the addition of two words: "I said."

It would go like this: Pop would say, "Vinny, help your mother with the dishes." There would be a slight hesitation on my part followed by an audible sigh, "Ah, Pop…"

If my father was in a playful mood, he might let me go on and even allow me to offer some feeble excuse as to why I couldn't help my mother with the dishes. But no matter where we were in the debate, all negotiations were over when I heard Pop say, "I SAID, help your mother with the dishes." End of discussion. *Fuhgeddaboudit.*

You may have heard alternate versions in your house. I had friends who said that their fathers would build slowly to a climactic silencer, using one or more of these sayings: "Because I said so," "Because I'm your father," "You're in my house," and, of course, "Don't make me come over there." In our house, we never got that far.

It is a wise child who knows his own father.
— Homer

If at first you don't succeed, do it like your mother told you.

— Unknown

A Higher Power

Things were different with my mother. In our family justice system, we had two separate but often equal branches. Pop laid down the law and carried out punishment. Mom maintained the law and let Pop think he held all the power.

If we disobeyed her, Mom had immense control over us. Sometimes, our actions were so monstrous that she disciplined us herself. But she always held the trump card, too: "Wait until your father gets home." These words cut into our souls, conjuring up that familiar fear and some pretty gruesome images. How we behaved the rest of the day was critical. If our remorse seemed genuine enough, Pop wouldn't hear about what we had done, and the punishment would not be revisited.

I don't want you to think a dark cloud of fear floated over our house. There was much more to our family structure than discipline. My father had a strong voice for common sense and living by our wits. My mother's voice was caring and nurturing and she taught us to live by The Golden Rule.

My point, and I do have one, is that being successful is as simple as being a positive and disciplined person. Negativity Management focuses on both attributes.

Dwelling on the negative simply contributes to
its power.

— Shirley MacLaine

Positives and Negatives – What a Charge

You may be wondering why you should spend time "managing negatives" instead of just creating more positives. Wouldn't it be easier to just give money to the Boy Scouts or something? In a nutshell: There are people who do nice things all the time, but they are still jerks. Positive actions hurt no one. I guess that's why they are positive. Negative actions hurt people whether we mean to or not, so focusing on eliminating negatives is more important in the big picture.

For you philosophical "Is the glass half-full or half-empty?" people (and Star Trek fans), let me put it another way. By not doing something negative, you are in fact doing something positive. When you eliminate something negative, the space that the negative occupied in the cosmos ceases to be and the positive takes over. Have I lost anyone?

I realize that evaluating positives and negatives can be subjective. For example, a person may think that applying makeup, painting letters on their bare chest, and spelling out words with their friends at a football game is a positive display of team support. Others could see this as a negative thing.

Doing the Two-Step

What's important is that you focus on analyzing your own life and acting accordingly. Let's revisit my two-step program:

- Step 1: Get off your butt. *Analyze your life.*
- Step 2. Do something. *Act accordingly.*

A Positive Example:

The last part of my book – the workbook section – is a testament to my own Negativity Management philosophy. I developed it after noticing the confused looks in the audience every time I introduced the theory. Here's how I applied the two-step program:

- Step 1: I *analyzed* the situation to identify the negative impact on my life – the confused individuals in my audience.
- Step 2: I *acted accordingly* by developing a tool these individuals can use to apply my theory to their own lives while I sell a book.

Because I do not have to master Negativity Management to be successful, I am a better person simply because I applied the theory, even if the workbook doesn't help my audience. However, because you're reading this, I know that someone paid for my workbook. That means that my actions benefited me even if they haven't benefited you – yet. So that's good, that's positive.

You see, if I'm happy, everyone around me is happier. Conversely, if I'm acting in a negative fashion, the effect on the people I come in contact with is negative.

Each of us affects the lives of so many people. I don't want to get all "George Bailey" from *It's a Wonderful Life* on you here, but we come in contact with a lot of people who in turn come in contact with a lot of people, and people who need people are… Wait a minute, I'm mixing my metaphors. But you get the picture.

Do THIS

One starts an action simply because one must do something.

— T.S. Eliot

To do is to be.

— Socrates

To be is to do.

— Plato

The way to do is to be.

— Lao-tzu

Try not. Do or do not. There is no try.

— Yoda

PART IV:

The Negativity Management Workbook

Once you replace negative thoughts with positive ones, you'll start having positive results.

— Willie Nelson

By now I hope you're feeling motivated, because it's time to put down that cheese and get to work on your life. Don't worry – with my simple two-step program, you'll be done by lunch.

> *Goals are dreams with deadlines.*
> — Diana Scharf Hunt

Using Your Workbook

This workbook serves as your own personal Negativity Management tool. Simply follow these instructions when completing the exercises:

1. **Use a pen, not a pencil.** Your first thoughts are the most important, so you won't get an accurate analysis if you erase them.

   Note: Many of you will want to measure your progress by performing the exercises again and again. Additional copies of this workbook can be purchased online at www.motivatethis.net. Remember that it's a federal offense to copy this book, in part or in whole. More importantly, it offends me.

2. **Be honest when you record your answers.** There are no right or wrong answers, and I'm not here to judge you. Every person will respond differently, so honesty is all that counts.

Practicing Negativity Management

> *Positive anything is better than negative thinking.*
> — Elbert Hubbard

I've developed four exercises that are simple and make sense. The goal is to tip your life scale in the positive direction. As a result of completing these tasks, you'll be a much better, happier person, which will encourage you to do more positive things to keep tipping the scale.

When there are no more positives to add, start eliminating negatives. Doing so also tips the scale in your favor toward the positive.

Look at it this way: Imagine an old-fashioned balance scale with two plates, like the scales of justice. One plate represents the negative things in your life; the other plate represents the positive things. If you do something positive…that side gets heavier and the positive plate moves down, tipping the scale in your favor. By the same token, if you eliminate something negative, that side gets lighter and you achieve the same results.

Accentuate the positive and eliminate the negative – it's simple. So if you can't move the scales in your favor…if you can't see results, it's not my fault. Only you can choose to make solid changes in your life. End of discussion. All together now? *Fuhgeddaboudit.*

> *Things do not change, we change.*
> — Henry David Thoreau

Accentuate the **P**ositive, **E**liminate the **N**egative

Tip the scales in your favor and check your progress often. You'll be amazed how quickly you see results. Of course, they could be negative results but, by checking often, you can make adjustments.

> *Map out your future, but do it in pencil.*
> — Jon Bon Jovi

Exercise Instructions:
In each of the following exercises, apply my two-step program to analyze the situation and act accordingly. *Remember, with the two-step program, any progress is considered success and you should celebrate.*

EXERCISE 1: Emphasize Your Positives

> *A positive attitude may not solve all your problems, but it will annoy enough people to make it worth the effort.*
>
> — Herm Albright

Step 1: List five positive things about yourself.

1. _____

2. _____

3. _____

4. _____

5. _____

Step 2: Whenever possible, accentuate these positive things to everyone you meet and keep up the good work. When you feel that you've gotten as much play out of these things as you can, start a new list.

> *Nothing is permanent but change.*
>
> — Heraclitus

Exercise Tip: We all like to talk about our accomplishments and the good things that have happened to us, but be careful with the way you express yourself. No one likes a braggart or a sore winner. When completing Step 2 of this exercise, practice subtlety and humility.

Observations:
During this exercise, I learned:

_____

_____

_____

_____

_____

Dream THIS

Shoot for the moon. Even if you miss, you'll land among the stars.

— Les Brown

Dream as if you'll live forever; live as if you'll die tomorrow.

— James Dean

When your heart is in your dream, no request is too extreme.

— Jiminy Cricket

EXERCISE 2: Set New Goals

> *You must have long-range goals to keep you from being frustrated by short-range failures.*
> — Charles C. Noble

Step 1(a): List five things you hope to accomplish. These can be short-term and/or long-term goals, but they should be positive things.

1. ─────────────────────────────────

2. ─────────────────────────────────

3. ─────────────────────────────────

4. ─────────────────────────────────

5. ─────────────────────────────────

Step 1(b): List five positive things you feel like you'll never accomplish.

1. ─────────────────────────────────

2. ─────────────────────────────────

3. ─────────────────────────────────

4. ─────────────────────────────────

5. ─────────────────────────────────

Step 2: It's nice to have goals. Share these goals with others to show them that you strive to be a better person.

Exercise Tip: The fact that you may never be able to accomplish the items listed in Step 1(b) doesn't mean that you shouldn't think about them. If enough of us focus on impossible accomplishments, we may all come closer to attaining the unattainable. If visualization really works, you'll be ahead of the game.

Since everyone else is doing it, let me borrow from a cartoon to illustrate my point (like a real motivational guru): Peter Pan had to think of positive things in order to fly. Get it?

Observations:
During this exercise, I learned:

_____

_____

_____

_____

_____

> *I have not failed. I've just found 10,000 ways that won't work.*
> — Thomas Edison

EXERCISE 3: Whack the Negative

> *Reality is the best possible cure for dreams.*
> — Roger Starr

Eliminating the negative is harder than emphasizing the positive because negatives seem so much more abundant. That's why this exercise is a three-parter.

PART 1: Focus on Your Life

Step 1: List the top five negative outside forces affecting your life.

Note: Although people can be negative forces, do not list individuals below. We will deal with them later in the Bonus Exercise. For this exercise, concentrate on negatives like finances, traffic, shopping – you know, everyday "BS."

1. _____

2. _____

3. _____

4. _____

5. _____

Step 2(a): Review your list for negative things that are beyond your control.

- If any item falls into this "nothing you can do about it" category, write an "N" next to it.
- Reconsider each item you've marked with an "N." If there is truly no way for you to affect the negative, cross it off your list and learn to adapt.

Example: Unless you leave for work before 5:00 a.m. and come home after 9:00 p.m., traffic is a negative reality that is beyond your control. It has an extremely negative effect on people, but there's nothing we can do about it. However, the way we choose to deal with that reality is up to us. Keep this example in mind as you review your list.

> *Life is a shipwreck but we must not forget to sing in the lifeboats.*
>
> — Voltaire

Step 2(b): Consider each of the remaining items. These negative forces in your life *can* be influenced by what you say and do. In some way, you may even contribute to these negatives.

- Identify at least one thing that you can do to avoid, affect, or preferably eliminate the negative. Be creative. How can you make the experience or force more palatable, even enjoyable? Do this with each of the items on your list. Record your action plan on the lines provided.
- Put your plan into action, crossing items off the list as you conquer them.
- When the list is "rubbed out," start a new list. This is an ongoing process and, every time you clean the slate, you should reward yourself. Then write down five more negative forces in your life.

Action Plan:

_____

_____

_____

_____

Exercise Tip: There's not enough time in the day to deal with everything in your life, so it only makes sense to let go of those things in your life that are negative.

Observations:
During this part of the exercise, I learned:

_____

_____

_____

_____

If you don't think every day is a good day, just try missing one.
—Cavett Robert

PART 2: Focus on Others

Step 1: List the top five negative things others do that tick you off. *For the sake of time, please only list five. I know there are more, but let's begin with a short list.*

1. _____

2. _____

3. _____

4. _____

5. _____

Step 2: Consider each item on the list.
- Is there any way that you can tactfully approach the person to point out the negativity of this action?
- If you are successful in eliminating some negative qualities in others, reward yourself by adding new items to your list (you'll need a new workbook, of course).

Exercise Tip: Be careful when completing Step 2 of this exercise. Sometimes all people need is for someone to help them open their eyes, but we don't want them to blacken yours.

Keep in mind that an individual may not be receptive to criticism. When you call someone on a negative behavior, the result can be anything from acceptance to violence to alienation to sleeping on the couch. Test the waters before confronting someone on a negative trait that bothers you and others.

Example:

Let's say Bob has a habit of belching real loud after he finishes a beer. You can say to Bob just after such a belch, "Bob, are you aware that you belch every time you finish a beer?" Keep a close eye on Bob's expression and let his reaction guide your next steps.

If Bob replies with something like, "No, really, every time? I wasn't aware of that. Do you think other people notice?" He is open to suggestion and you can proceed with something like, "I'm sure they do. Is it something you think you can control?" Bob, not feeling threatened in this scenario continues, "I'll try to be more conscious of it. Gee, thanks."

However, if Bob is not open to criticism at this time, the scenario may play out this way:

YOU: Bob, are you aware that you belch every time you finish a beer?

BOB: Yeah? What the *?/!%* is it to you?

YOU: Nothing, I think it's way cool. Maybe sometime you can teach me how you do that.

Part of practicing Negativity Management is evaluating when someone is receptive to change and choosing the best course of action.

> *Things turn out best for the people who make the best out of the way things turn out.*
> — Art Linkletter

Observations:
During this part of the exercise, I learned:

_____

_____

_____

_____

_____

PART 3: Focus on You

Now we come to the most difficult task in Negativity Management: identifying the negative traits that YOU possess. We all have them – believe me, I know. It's easy to see the negative in others...but look inside? We don't always see ourselves the way others see us.

Step 1: List the top five negative things about yourself. *Be honest.*

1. _____

2. _____

3. _____

4. _____

5. _____

Step 2: Rank each item on your list based on how hard it would be to eliminate these negative traits, to just "whack 'em."

- Assign a number to each item – 1 being the easiest to obliterate and 5 being the most difficult. Don't get discouraged by the results.
- Identify things that you can do to eliminate each of the items on your list. Record your action plan on the lines provided.
- Focus on eliminating the items ranked "1" first, then "2" then "3," and so on. By starting with the easier traits, you will succeed early, feel positive about the results, and have the motivation to carry on to the more difficult traits.

Action Plan:

_____

_____

_____

Exercise Tip: Remember that, when practicing Negativity Management, any little thing you do helps make you a more positive and, therefore, better person. For example, let's say you use the "F" word three hundred times a day. If you eliminate one hundred utterances of the word, even if no one else seems to notice, you're doing a good thing.

> *Flaming enthusiasm, backed up by horse sense and persistence, is the quality that most frequently makes for success.*
>
> — Dale Carnegie

Observations:
During this part of the exercise, I learned:

_____

_____

_____

_____

_____

Extra Credit:
The next page has been intentionally left blank in case you want to continue your list. *It also helps to pad the book.*

If you cannot identify any additional negative traits, pinch yourself to wake up. You're dreaming.

> *If at first you don't succeed, skydiving is not for you.*
> — Arthur McAuliff

Extra Credit Workspace

EXERCISE 4: Latch onto Somebody Cool

Congratulations – you've made it through the tough stuff. This exercise is the easiest.

> *The most important single influence in the life of a person is another person...who is worthy of emulation.*
> — Paul D. Shafer

Step 1(a): Identify ten people you admire. Write down their names and specific things they have said or done that you feel are positive.

1. _____

2. _____

3. _____

4. _____

5. _____

6. _____

7. _____

8. _____

9. _____

10. _____

Step 1(b): Review your list now and rewrite it, this time ranking items in order of importance ("1" being the most important and "10" the least).

1. _____

2. _____

3. _____

4. _____

5. _____

6. _____

7. _____

8. _____

9. _____

10. _____

> *As you get older it is harder to have heroes, but it is sort of necessary.*
>
> — Ernest Hemingway

Step 2(a): Latch onto these people and copy their actions.

- Look at the top five items on the list you developed in Step 1(b).
- Imitate these positive deeds by doing the same thing, or at least saying something positive about the person/good deed.
- Repeat this step with the second five items on your list.

Step 2(b): If any of the people on this list are local, schedule a "sit down" with them.

- Take them to lunch or buy them a cup of espresso. (None of this Starbucks crap, either – real espresso served by a real Italian.)
- Tell these people that you respect them and ask for any advice about becoming a better person. By stroking their ego, you'll be surprised to see how giving people are, especially when you're paying.

Exercise Tip: There are people all around you doing positive things. As an ongoing practice, say nice things about these people and praise their work. What you're doing is affirming the positive in others, latching onto it, and taking a free ride. This practice makes everyone involved feel good, and that's positive.

> *There is a difference between imitating a good man and counterfeiting him.*
> — Benjamin Franklin

Observations:

During this exercise, I learned:

_____

_____

_____

_____

_____

Additional Notes:

_____

_____

_____

_____

_____

_____

_____

_____

_____

_____

BONUS EXERCISE: Quest for the Positive

If you feel that you have mastered the practice of Negativity Management, you're ready for this exercise.

> *I just need somewhere to dump all my negativity.*
> — Van Morrison

Step 1(a): Make a list of the three people that you dislike the most.

Note: Use code names so you do not reveal their true identities in case your workbook falls into the wrong hands. In fact, it may be a good idea to destroy this book once you're finished. (You can always buy another one at www.motivatethis.net.)

Top Three People You Dislike:

1.————————————————————————

2.————————————————————————

3.————————————————————————

Step 1(b): Under each name, write the three things that you most dislike about the person. Start with the person you dislike the least and build up to the one you dislike the most. This is the most fun part of the exercise.

First Person_____

Negative Traits:

1. _____

2. _____

3. _____

Second Person_____

Negative Traits:

1. _____

2. _____

3. _____

Third Person_____

Negative Traits:

1. _____

2. _____

3. _____

Step 2: Here comes the hard part. Write three things about each person that are *positive*. Give yourself a time limit on this one – let's say two minutes per person. *Start now.*

First Person_____
Positive Traits:

1._____

2._____

3._____

Time's up! If you couldn't think of three positive things in these two minutes, don't give this person another thought. They are not worth your time. Move on and do the same with the other two people on your list.

> *If you can't say anything nice about a person, don't say anything at all.*
> — Most everyone's mother

Second Person_____
Positive Traits:

1._____

2._____

3._____

Third Person_____
Positive Traits:

1._____

2._____

3._____

> **Exercise Tip:** Did you notice how much easier it was to come up with three negative things about others? It probably made you feel better than when you had to think about your own negative traits. You should understand at this point in your study of Negativity Management, though, that you must first *identify* the negative in order to manage it.

Observations:
During this exercise, I learned:

_____

_____

_____

_____

_____

> *Swallow a toad in the morning and you will encounter nothing more disgusting the rest of the day.*
> — Nicolas de Chamfort

GROUP EXERCISE: *The Fava Factor*

Here's the final challenge for those of you who are studying Negativity Management in a workshop-type setting.

Rather than pointing out your own negatives and the negatives of the people in the group around you right now, apply Negativity Management to someone I know. Someone who doesn't know where you live.

Step 1: Read the following story together.

There's this guy I know. John Michael Fava. He was the coolest guy I ever met. He talked cool, dressed cool, and had a way with the ladies. Every guy wanted to be John Michael Fava.

One day, Fava's at the 2001 Odyssey disco. He's dancing up a storm with his favorite partner, Maria, doing all these John Travolta moves. He does this squat thing and his pants rip. He tries to recover quickly and drops Maria. She goes rolling off this platform and Fava falls on his butt, only his butt falls into a full tray of drinks. As John was way too cool to wear underwear, he now has broken glass stuck in his butt.

They had to carry him out on a stretcher with his derriere in the air. Everyone was staring, pointing, laughing. I could have sworn I saw one of those cocktail umbrellas sticking up amongst the shards of glass.

Now that's all anyone ever remembers about John Michael Fava.

Step 2: Clearly, John did not apply my two-step program to his situation (particularly Step 1). Use the following discussion questions to prompt conversation about how John could have applied Negativity Management and how you can learn from his mistakes.

Discussion Questions:
- What could John do to find the positive in this situation? *(Hint: It rhymes with "move to another state.")*
- What negatives could John have eliminated before the incident that may have prevented the outcome? How? *(Hint: Follow Mom's advice to always wear clean underwear in case you have an accident.)*
- What negatives could John have eliminated after the incident? *(Hint: It also rhymes with "move to another state." The lesson here is that, when there is no positive, eliminating the negative IS the positive.)*
- How does John's situation relate to your own life?

Exercise Tip: People only tend to remember the stupid things you do. If you screw up and do something stupid, really negative, you have to do some damage control, fast. If you don't put a positive spin on your situation immediately, the stupid things you do can follow you the rest of your life – just like me. I mean "John."

If at first you don't succeed, try, try again. Then give up. There's no use in being a damn fool about it.
— W. C. Fields

Observations:
During this exercise, I learned:

_____

_____

_____

_____

_____

Conclusion

Hopefully you see that you can apply all of these exercises to your life again and again in varying degrees. They are simple and they make sense. By completing these tasks, you will continue to tip your life scale toward the positive. Don't forget that it is equally important to emphasize the positives and eliminate the negatives to keep the scale tipping in your favor.

I know I said that I'm not here to judge you, but that doesn't mean I wouldn't like to. Write to me with questions about your exercise results – and any other question for that matter. I'll judge you and then give you my advice. Go to my Web site at www.motivatethis.net and click on "Dear Vinny."

> *If at first you don't succeed, destroy all evidence that you tried.*
> — Unknown (My favorite author)

THE LAST WORD

If a book or speech is crafted well, you can be moved to tears. You may even be moved to action, sometimes with negative results. But are you truly motivated? The truth is...now pay attention cause this sentence sums up the entire book...The truth is no man, or woman, can motivate you. Only YOU can motivate you.

You can see the best speakers, read the best books, listen to the best tapes; hey, you may have even read something in this book that made sense (stranger things have happened). But unless YOU make the choice to do something about it, nothing is going to happen. Nothing is going to change. It's all up to you.

I hope I've given you some good laughs and positive thoughts. But if I didn't, that's okay, too, because the book is paid for – and that's good, that's positive. I mean, even if you stole the book, the person you stole it from paid for it. If the person you stole it from liked it, they'll buy another copy at www.motivatethis.net.

I leave you with these final thoughts: Instead of looking at someone and thinking, "What are our differences?" you should consider, "In what ways are we the same?" The French, of course, say *vive la difference*. But remember, that's the French saying that.

Sure, it's okay to be different. But we spend so much time identifying our differences that we don't take time to celebrate our similarities.

Always look for the positive in someone. If you look for it, you will find it. You will be surprised to learn how much you have in common with your fellow man, or woman. But, if you ever come across a person and you try and you try and you try to find the positive and there is none... dial 9-1-1 and run like hell.

End of discussion. *Fuhgeddaboudit.*

Ciao for now!

Vinny

Coming soon from Vinny Verelli...
I GOT YOUR CHICKEN SOUP RIGHT HERE
(It's what you call an anthology.)

THE LAST LAUGH

All this talk about negativity can be a real bummer –
that's why it's so important to laugh.

The most wasted of all days is one without laughter.
— e.e. cummings

Laughter is the shortest distance between two people.
— Victor Borge

*When people are laughing, they're generally not
killing each other.*
— Alan Alda

Laughter is a tranquilizer with no side effects.
— Arnold Glasow

*I am thankful for laughter, except when milk comes
out of my nose.*
— Woody Allen

If you bought the stuff in this book,
can I interest you in a bridge?

Vinny is available to speak to your business or organization. To learn more, visit www.motivatethis.net.

LaVergne, TN USA
28 December 2009
168192LV00001B/4/A